Date: 11/4/21

BR 553.7 STE
Stephenchel, Tora,
Cold water /

BY TORA STEPHENCHEL

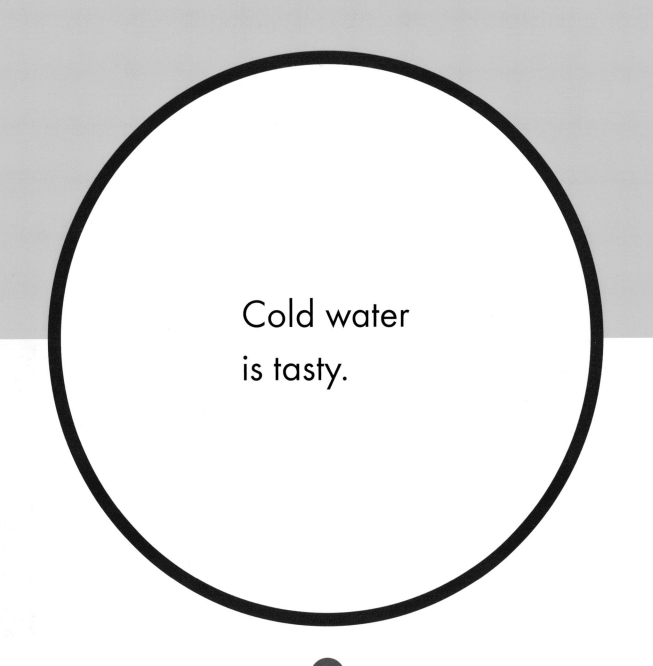

Cold water
is tasty.

Cold water
helps me clean.

Cold water
is good for plants.

Cold water
is good for pets.

Cold water
can make ice.

Cold water
can make snow.

Cold water
is in rivers and lakes.

Cold water
is in the ocean.

Cold water
falls from the sky.

Cold water
is almost everywhere!

Note to Caregivers and Educators

Sight words are a foundation for reading. It's important for young readers to have sight words memorized at a glance without breaking them down into individual letter sounds. Sight words are often phonetically irregular and can't be sounded out, so readers need to memorize them. Knowing sight words allows readers to focus on more difficult words in the text. The intent of this book is to repeat specific sight words as many times as possible throughout the story. Through repetition of the words, emerging readers will recognize, and ideally memorize, each sight word. Memorizing sight words can help improve readers' literacy skills.

cold

water

23

About the Author

Tora Stephenchel lives in Minnesota. She loves to spend time with her son, daughter, husband, and two silly dogs.

Published by The Child's World®
1980 Lookout Drive • Mankato, MN 56003-1705
800-599-READ • www.childsworld.com

Photographs © Alex Staroseltsev/Shutterstock.com: 23; Alex_Ugalek/Shutterstock.com: 9; caifas/Shutterstock.com: 5; Dave Pot/Shutterstock.com: cover, 1; Dmitry Naumov/Shutterstock.com: 21; Evgeny Atamanenko/Shutterstock.com: 18; Maximus Art/Shutterstock.com: 6; MH Anderson Photography/Shutterstock.com: 14;Stivog/Shutterstock.com: 2; Valentyn Volkov/Shutterstock.com: 10; Willyam Bradberry/Shutterstock.com: 17; Yuliya Evstratenko/Shutterstock.com: 13

ISBN 9781503845039 (Reinforced Library Binding)
ISBN 9781503846524 (Portable Document Format)
ISBN 9781503847712 (Online Multi-user eBook)
LCCN 2020931153

Printed in the United States of America